Don't Make Me Rattle!

by
Elaine A. Powers

Illustrated by
Nicholas Thorpe

Don't Make Me Rattle!

by Elaine A. Powers
Copyright 2018 by Elaine A. Powers
All rights reserved.

ISBN-13: 978-1985736610
ISBN-10: 1985736616

Published by Lyric Power Publishing LLC, Tucson AZ

All information provided is believed and intended to be reliable, but accuracy cannot be guaranteed by the author or the publisher.

DON'T MAKE ME RATTLE

by
Elaine A. Powers

Illustrated by
Nicholas Thorpe

Don't Make Me Rattle! But if you do,
Remember, it's only a warning to you.

3

We're here on the ground, roaming around,
Where dangers like being stepped on really abound.
Some people think we want to do battle,
They become afraid when they hear us rattle.

"Let me kill it," the person begs,
"It eats my chickens and some of her eggs.
They're treacherous creatures, with no earthly use!"
They think that killing us cannot be abuse.

7

But we do have our uses, believe me, it's true.
I'll tell you about them, so you'll think so too.
If you get to know me, you won't be afraid
You'll want to protect me and come to my aid.

8

9

I, a rattlesnake, like all reptiles, am called ectotherm,
A fancy term for "cold-blooded" that all should learn.
I depend on the environment to keep my body warm,
Using the sun and shadow, my temp to transform.

Our genus names, *Crotalus* and *Sistrurus*, are from Greek,
Rattling like castanets and sistrums is how we speak.
The rattle you see at my tail's end,
Is made from hollow, interlocking rings of keratin.

These modified scales so unique to rattlers' tails
Are made from the same protein as your fingernails.
Special muscles cause the rings to vibrate
Over fifty times per second, an incredible rate.

11

We hold our rattles up, since they are easy to break.
But scales still come off, leaving pieces in our wake.
So you can't use the rattle to determine our ages.
Our size and our gender are much better gauges.

It's not just our rattles that make people wary,
Some think that our faces are also quite scary.
Our triangular heads are shaped like an arrow,
The pupils of our eyes are vertical and narrow.

Called pit vipers, we have two facial pits,
Little depressions where heat-sensing organs sit.
Located between our nostrils and eyes
Is where these infrared imagers lie.

We use a thermal image to detect our meal
And track its location, for us, not a big deal.
We're mostly nocturnal but can be active by day,
We're ambush hunters, lying in wait for our prey.

Rattlers have tongues that we flick out and back.
We're not smelling your scent so we can attack.
We're "tasting" the molecules that float in the air,
Our Jacobson's organs determine who or what is there.

We haven't got ears and can't really "hear,"
But we sense sound vibrations when someone is near.

What is our prey, you might want to ask?
Insects, birds, rodents, and reptiles who bask.
How do we eat our various quarry?
We swallow them whole, so it's not at all gory.

We have fangs in our mouths that fold back,
Then snap out and upright when we attack.
The hinge on the top of our mouth has allowed
Us with the longest snake fangs to be endowed.

You see, our fangs are tapered and hollow
To inject a toxin that helps us swallow.
The venom we inject is a digestive aid,
Like people's saliva – that's why it's made.

We have no teeth designed for chewing;
The venom makes food softer – that's what it's doing.
Our venom has proteins to stop and digest our prey,
And we swallow head first so limbs don't get in the way.

19

Venom is also a built-in defense—
To avoid being bitten, use good sense.
Don't step on, pick up, or handle us,
And we won't strike at you or cause a fuss.

Rattlers cause most snake bites, though few people die.
The location of most bites will leave you asking "why?"
Though on the ground is a rattler's usual place,
Most bites occur on men's hands or face.

Not all our bites contain venom, they're called dry.
That's interesting, you cannot deny.

Being picked up only makes us scared.
Leave us alone and no fangs will be bared.

A venomous bite is not our only protection
Camouflage colors help us avoid detection.

Males must show strength to attract a mate.
In combat dances they will participate.
Extending their bodies upward, they intertwine and sway,
Then push on each other until one slithers away.

22

How we rattlers drink raindrops is really quite cool,
We coil our bodies and let the water pool.

A mother rattler keeps her babies inside,
No nest is needed when there are no eggs to hide.
Many mothers congregate before they give birth,
Gathering in a den nestled in the earth.
In summer, when the babies are ready to hatch,
The mother gives live birth to the entire batch.

The kids don't leave Mama right away;
The neonates stay by her and don't go astray
Until they shed, then away they slither
To find their own territories, yon and hither.

24

Baby rattlers start out about a foot long,
Though they're small, their venom is quite strong.
Babies have only a button at their tail's end;
They must shed first for their rattling to begin.

Daughters may use their mother's den,
Rattlers also baby-sit for each other now and then.

When we hibernate or bromate, we gather together.
It's how we survive in winter's cold weather.
Gravid females may stay in the den to give birth;
Families return each year to the same patch of earth.

27

These dens, or hibernacula, are sites of social interaction.
Seeing us gathered, people feel a negative reaction.
But we rattlesnakes don't spend this time alone!
Tortoises, mammals, and lizards call these dens home.

You may think it strange to find us together,
But that is what happens in cold weather.
A group of us is called a "rhumba" of rattlesnakes.
But I prefer a "snuggle" of rattlers and hope it takes.

29

Rattlers have predators, I tell you it's true,
Many other animals dine on us, too,
Roadrunners, coyotes, and kingsnakes to name a few.
These hunters are clever and know what to do.

It's a dangerous world I'm sorry to say;
Very few rattlers see their second birthday.

We avoid places where lots of people appear,
Preferring undisturbed land in which to disappear.
Left on our own, we may live over thirty years,
But dealing with people is our greatest fear.

Men come hunting us for round-ups and massive killing;
Vast numbers of dead snakes become trophies – it's chilling!

Gasoline is poured into our dens to force us out.
Gas kills those other animals, too, have no doubt.
To read of such cruel activities may make you tense,
But together we can end such horrible events.

Along with deliberate killing, we die in other ways as well.
Dogs attack us, but can be trained to avoid our smell.
Many rattlers are run over and end up dead on roads,
And people kill us with shovels at their abodes.

Habitat destruction hurts us as our dens become cities,
But we also suffer from negative publicity.
Entire populations have been killed from ignorance.
We're not cute and furry, so we don't stand a chance.

If all rattlesnakes were killed, why should you care?
Many think life would be better without us there.

Whoa, that's not true, you don't know all we do.
We eat lots of disease-toting rodents to protect you.

Eating tick-carrying rats and mice is a vital role;
We help keep Lyme Disease and Plague under control.
We sometimes "rescue" seeds that rodents ate that day,
Dispersing these undigested seeds along our way.

Scientists study rattlers to find important answers,
Drugs from our venom treat heart disease and cancers!

Rattlesnakes don't want to harm you or your pet,
Being aggressive is not our mindset.
I'd much rather hide from you than do battle,
So, please, stay away and...

Don't Make Me Rattle!

Acknowledgments

Living in the Sonoran Desert, I share my yard and garage with Western Diamondback Rattlesnakes. One of my goals for the Don't series is to help people learn about animals that may be misunderstood. James Jarchow, DVM, suggested I write one about rattlesnakes. I agreed immediately because I was too familiar with the negative attitudes expressed toward these amazing reptiles.

Melissa Amarello, co-founder and Director of Education of Advocates for Snake Preservation, studies rattlesnake behavior and provided fascinating information about their social lives and corrected me when my information went astray.

As always, Pamela Bickell, Kate J. Steele, Susan M. Oyler, Brad Peterson and his daughter Ellie provided valuable insight. I couldn't create these books without my editors Annie Maier and Nora Miller.

My thanks to the rattlers in my yard for keeping the rodents under control and bringing enjoyment to my wildlife viewing by their presence. All rattlesnakes are welcome and I appreciate being warned when I walk too close. I will try to not make the rattlesnakes rattle.

Made in the USA
San Bernardino, CA
14 March 2018